Discovering

OWLS

Robert Burton

The Bookwright Press
New York · 1990

Discovering Nature

First published in the
United States in 1990 by
The Bookwright Press
387 Park Avenue South
New York, NY 10016

First published in 1989 by
Wayland (Publishers) Limited
61 Western Road, Hove
East Sussex BN3 1JD, England

© Copyright 1989 Wayland (Publishers) Limited

Frontispiece *These two young screech owls still have their downy gray feathers.*

Cover *A young barn owl. These owls are becoming quite rare in Europe.*

Typeset by DP Press Limited, Sevenoaks, Kent
Printed in Italy by G. Canale & C. S.p.A. - Turin

Library of Congress Cataloging-in-Publication Data
Burton, Robert, 1941–
   Discovering owls/by Robert Burton.
     p. cm. — (Discovering nature)
   Summary: An introduction to the physical characteristics, habits, natural environment, and relationship to human beings of the owl.
   Bibliography: p.
   Includes index.
   ISBN 0–531–18318–1
   1. Owls—Juvenile literature.   [1. Owls.]   I. Title.
II. Series.
QL696.S83B87   1990
598′.97—dc20   89–9708
                                      CIP
                                      AC

Contents

1
Introducing Owls

All owls look much the same. This great gray owl shows their typical glaring eyes and upright posture.

What Are Owls?

Owls are easy to recognize because their shape is unlike that of any other bird. The head is very large and has a thick covering of feathers, so there does not seem to be a neck. Owls perch with their backs very straight. Their round, glaring eyes are set in the front of the face, instead of at the sides of the head, as in most birds. This gives owls a very human appearance. Many owls have a wide ring of feathers around each eye, which makes them look as if they are wearing spectacles. The two rings together are called the facial disks.

Owls are **birds of prey**. They are armed with sharp, curved **talons** for catching their prey and short, hooked beaks for killing the prey and tearing its flesh. Owls are not related to eagles, hawks and falcons, which are also birds of prey with sharp talons and bills. Most owls are **nocturnal**, which means that they fly and hunt at night. The other kinds of birds of prey hunt by day. Owls are not brightly colored, although some are white. **Species** of owls that live in the woods are usually dark brown or gray, while those seen in open country have a paler **plumage**.

Below *A barn owl flies silently in the dark to search for its next meal.*

An owl uses its needle-sharp talons to catch its prey.

Some Kinds of Owls

Owls are found in every part of the world, except Antarctica and a few islands in the middle of oceans. There are 133 species known to **ornithologists**, but new species are still sometimes discovered in remote places. Most species live in warm countries.

The largest owls are the eagle owls. They grow up to 73 cm (29 in) from head to tail. The smallest owls are the little owls, pygmy owls and elf owls. The smallest of all is the least pygmy owl of South America. It is 12 cm (4.7 in) long – smaller than a sparrow.

Some owls have "ears," which are not real ears but tufts of feathers on the top of the bird's head. Some

Barn owls are rather different from other owls. They have a heart-shaped facial disk and a thin beak.

ornithologists believe these "ears" may help owls recognize each other. The long-eared and short-eared owls are similar in appearance, but the long-eared owl lives in woods, while the short-eared owl lives in open country.

Although all owls are very much alike in their appearance, the eight species of barn owls and two species of bay owls are rather different. They can be distinguished from other owls by their smaller eyes and heart-shaped facial disks. These owls live in open country. They have longer legs than most owls and can run well. The barn owl lives in more parts of the world than almost any other bird. It is found on every continent except Antarctica, and its habit of nesting in farm buildings makes it well known.

The "ears" of this long-eared owl are only tufts of feathers. They are not used for hearing.

2
Living in the Dark

Owls have very sharp eyesight, so they can fly among trees and spot their prey when it is very dark.

Seeing

Most owls are especially adapted to flying and hunting in the dark. They can see well enough to fly through a wood when it is so dim that it looks pitch black to human eyes. There are two reasons why owls can see so well in the dark.

They have large **pupils**, which open wide at night to let as much light as possible into the eye. During the day the pupils close and shut out the bright light. The same happens in a cat's eyes, except that the owl's eyes close to a dot instead of a slit during the day.

Light entering the eye shines on the **retina** at the back of the eyeball where light detectors change it into nerve messages, which go to the brain. The owl's retina is very sensitive to dim light because it is packed with many more light detectors than the eyes of other animals. A tawny owl, which is strictly nocturnal, has eyes that are two or three times more sensitive than a human's eyes. However, a pygmy owl, which hunts by day, cannot see as well as a human at night.

The eyeballs of an owl are very large and can hardly move in their sockets. So, to look around, an owl has to turn its head. Some owls can twist their heads around until they are looking straight behind them.

Owls are unlike other birds because their eyes face forward. This helps them to tell exactly where their prey is, so they can pounce straight onto it. Some owls bob up and down or move their heads from side to side, which also helps them to judge distances.

Like other owls, the tawny owl can look all around. It turns its head until it can see over its back.

Hearing

Sharp hearing is even more important than keen eyesight for hunting in the dark. Faint rustlings and high-pitched squeaks are enough to give away mice and other **rodents** to an owl flying overhead or perched on a branch.

An owl's hearing is about ten times more sensitive than a human's, but it cannot hear high-pitched sounds as well. The hearing of a barn owl is so sensitive that it can pounce on a mouse in pitch darkness.

When an owl is listening for prey, it is helped by stiff feathers on the edge of the facial disk, which guide sound waves into the large ear openings. By moving the feathers on the facial disk, the owl concentrates on sounds from

Using its sharp sense of hearing, an American saw-whet owl pounces on a deer mouse in complete darkness.

different directions, in much the same way as a cat or dog turns its ears to listen carefully. The unusual position of the ear openings also helps the owl to tell exactly where any sounds are coming from.

The barn owl needs to hear only two sounds from a mouse. When it hears the first sound it turns its head to face roughly in the right direction. The second sound tells the owl exactly where the mouse is, and it can then pounce with pinpoint precision. Hunting becomes difficult in the rain because the sound of raindrops hitting the ground drowns the noises that the prey is making.

The opening of an owl's ear is hidden by its feathers. The stiff feathers around the ear guide sound waves into the opening, helping the owl to pinpoint its prey.

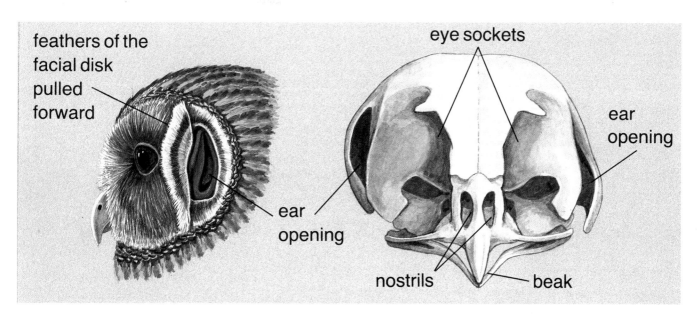

feathers of the facial disk pulled forward

ear opening

eye sockets

ear opening

nostrils

beak

Flying Quietly

Most birds of prey hunt either by waiting on a perch for prey to pass underneath or by flying close to the ground to search a large area. When the bird is perched, its prey has little chance of telling that danger is near, but the flapping of a bird's wings is very noisy. This is a disadvantage for a hunting bird that is trying to pounce on its victims before they can run

A barn owl glides effortlessly on its broad wings. The owl's silent flight helps it to surprise its prey.

away. Owls can approach their victims without disturbing them because they fly very quietly.

They fly effortlessly with their large, broad wings, which means that the wings make less noise than if they were flapping hard. Owls can also glide well, so they can skim over the ground with hardly a sound.

The flight of owls is made even quieter than that of other birds because their soft, fluffy-edged feathers deaden the noise of their movements through the air. Tests have shown that many of the animals that owls hunt cannot hear them approaching. Even so, some animals are good at escaping. The kangaroo rat, which lives in the deserts of the United States, has very sensitive ears. It can hear the faintest swish of an owl swooping toward it, and it quickly jumps out of the way.

When an owl has pinpointed the position of its prey, it dives toward it. The owl's aim is so accurate that its talons can pin the prey to the ground.

searching for prey   diving   striking

3
What Owls Eat

A tawny owl holds the body of a mouse under its talons and pulls off pieces of meat with its hooked beak.

Tawny Owls

The tawny owl lives in England mainly in the woods, but it also comes into towns and back yards. Unlike some other owls that come out during the day, the tawny owl is active almost always at night. Hunting starts a few minutes after sunset. Tawny owls are usually seen by day only when they have been disturbed.

Every tawny owl has a **territory** where it lives and hunts. By constantly hunting in the same area, the owl soon learns the best places to search for prey. It chases other tawny owls away from its territory, so that they cannot take its food.

A hunting territory is important for all species of owls. Tawny owl territories can be as small as 37 acres or as large as 500 acres. The actual size depends on the amount of prey in the area. If prey becomes rare, tawny owls lay fewer eggs and rear fewer young.

A tawny owl usually hunts by waiting on a perch and keeping watch for the sight or sound of its prey. Then it glides down swiftly and pounces. If the owl cannot see anything to catch, it soon moves to another perch and tries again. In open country, where there are fewer trees to perch on, the tawny owl often flies low over the ground in search of prey.

The tawny owl hunts mainly voles and mice, but it also catches a small number of birds by plucking them from their nests and roosts. It also lands and runs across the ground to catch beetles and earthworms. Even frogs and fish feature in the tawny owl's varied diet.

When young tawny owls first leave the nest they look gray and fluffy.

The female snowy owl has black bars on her white plumage. This makes her difficult to spot when she is sitting on her nest.

Snowy Owls

The snowy owl lives in the Arctic regions of Europe, Asia and North America, in treeless regions called tundra. It never gets dark during the Arctic summer when the snowy owl is nesting, so it has to hunt in daylight. The summer is very short, and snowy owls **migrate** southward to warmer countries to avoid the long Arctic winter.

Snowy owls hunt by perching on a boulder or hummock without moving, except to turn their heads and watch for prey. They eat any animals they can find, and they catch Arctic hares that can weigh 4 kg (9 lb), or over twice the weight of a snowy owl. They also catch many birds, up to the size of ducks, but their main prey is lemmings.

Lemmings are vole-like animals. They are usually caught as they run

over the ground, but they are not safe even when they hide under the snow. The number of lemmings on the tundra varies enormously from year to year. In some years they are very abundant; then the snowy owls have plenty of food and raise many young.

Snowy owls hunt lemmings and other animals in Arctic countries. Their white plumage conceals them against the snow.

In other years, lemmings are so scarce that the owls do not even try to nest and many fly south in search of food.

Eagle Owls

Eagle owls are the giants of the owl world. The largest eagle owls weigh 2–3 kg (4–6 lbs) or more and they have 1.5 m (5 ft) wingspans. Some make frightening shrieks.

Most of the twelve species of eagle owls live in Africa and Asia. There is one species in Europe. The great horned owl is the only eagle owl living in North America, and it is found all over the continent.

Eagle owls live in all sorts of countryside, from forests to deserts. Like the tawny owl, each eagle owl has a territory that is its hunting ground. The territory is about 10 km (6 mi) across and the eagle owl hunts

Eagle owls are the largest kind of owl. This European eagle owl has caught a rabbit, although it usually feeds on smaller animals.

by watching the ground from a perch for a few minutes. If it does not catch anything, it flies to the next perch.

Eagle owls eat anything from beetles to animals the size of a fox or a roe deer. These can be three or four times heavier than the eagle owl itself. They can kill large animals only if they catch them by surprise. Therefore, they eat mainly small animals.

The European eagle owl eats mostly voles, rats and mice, but it will also catch birds, frogs and even insects. The great horned owl eats large numbers of hares, as well as other animals. Eagle owls living near the ocean feed on ducks and puffins. The Akun eagle owl of African forests chases large flying insects in forest clearings.

The great horned owl is the only eagle owl to be found in North and South America.

Fishing Owls

There are seven species of fishing owls living in Africa and Asia. All seven are found along rivers, usually where they flow through forests. Fishing owls are related to the eagle owls but they have the habits of the fish-eating osprey.

Fishing owls are adapted for hunting prey that lives in water. Their feet are not feathered like those of other owls. They have very curved, sharp talons and spiny soles on their feet to help them seize and hold slippery fish.

They hunt by keeping watch from a perch overlooking shallow water. When they spot a fish or frog near the surface, they swoop down and snatch

A brown fishing owl waits on a rock. When it sees something to eat, it will swoop down and pluck it from the water.

it up without landing on the water.

Unlike other owls, fishing owls do not seem to have good hearing. This is not surprising because their underwater prey does not make a noise that they could hear. Neither can their prey hear them approaching, so there is no need for fishing owls to have soft feathers and fly silently like other owls.

Although the main prey of fishing owls is small fish, together with frogs and freshwater crabs, they also catch land animals such as mice, lizards and birds when they have the chance.

A fishing owl swoops to catch a fish. These owls live in forests in remote parts of the world, so their habits are rather a mystery to us.

The Smaller Owls

The burrowing owl, elf owl and little owl are three of the smallest owls. They spend more time on the ground than most owls. Compared with other owls, they have relatively long legs and can run well.

The burrowing owl lives in treeless, grassy country in the Americas, from the Great Plains of North America to the southern tip of South America. Several pairs may live close together, and each pair nests in a burrow originally made by another animal.

Burrowing owls start to hunt before

This burrowing owl lives in the grasslands of South Dakota. It nests in a hole in the ground.

nightfall and continue through the night. They chase flying insects, such as moths and beetles, and pounce on grasshoppers and caterpillars. Sometimes they follow horses to catch the insects that they disturb. They also hunt larger animals such as mice, small birds and lizards.

The elf owl is best known as an inhabitant of the deserts of the Southwest and Mexico, where it lives in giant saguaro cacti. But, it is also found in other habitats. It uses the abandoned nest holes of woodpeckers in saguaro cacti as well as other plants.

Elf owls hunt large insects, which they often catch in their talons while flying. Occasionally they catch rodents, birds, snakes and lizards.

The little owl of Europe eats mainly large insects and worms, which it often catches by running across the ground. However, it can also kill rats and small rabbits.

The European little owl flies down from its perch and chases small animals on the ground.

4
Owl Families

A pair of young barn owls have found a nesting hole. Once mated, they will stay together for life.

Courtship

In many species of owls, male and female stay together throughout the year. Young owls form new pairs and replace the older owls that have died during the winter.

Toward the end of winter, each pair of owls starts to make preparations for nesting. They become very noisy at this time of year. The male owl hoots to show other owls that he owns the territory. He has to stop other males from invading his territory and, if he has not got a mate, he has to attract a female. The male owl hoots either from perches in different parts of the territory or while flying around the territory.

Owls that are active by day make it clear which territory belongs to them. The long-eared owl and short-eared owl fly around their territories and clap their wings together loudly.

A pair of burrowing owls photographed near their nest hole. Sometimes several pairs of burrowing owls nest near one another.

Hooting and wing-clapping also help the males to attract females. Then the male and female get to know each other. Some male and female owls call together in "duets." The male tawny owl hoots and the female replies with a sharp "kewick."

Like many other kinds of birds, the male owl feeds the female when they are courting. This extra food helps to provide the female with the extra nourishment she needs to form the eggs in her body.

Nests and Eggs

Owls are not very good at making nests. Most owls make use of natural holes or take over the abandoned nests of other birds. If a tawny owl cannot find a natural hole in a tree, it will lay its eggs in the old nest of a crow, a hawk or a squirrel. Owls will regularly use the same nest year after year.

Owls living in open country nest on the ground. The snowy owl and short-eared owl make a shallow hole and sometimes line it with grass. The burrowing owl nests in an underground burrow originally made by a prairie dog, badger or other animal.

The barn owl gets its name from its habit of nesting in farm buildings, but it also uses houses and sometimes nests in trees.

Owls' eggs are white, and rounder than chickens' eggs. They are usually **incubated** only by the female. She rarely leaves the nest, and her mate brings her food.

Owls defend their nests against enemies, including humans. Those owls that nest in holes can be

Owl eggs are always white. These have been laid by a tawny owl in a nest that was once used by another bird.

dangerous because they attack with their talons when disturbed. They can blind a person who looks into the nest. Owls also defend their nests by trying to scare enemies. They fluff out their feathers and spread their wings

This Canadian short-eared owl is one of many kinds of owls that nest on the ground.

to make themselves look as large and fierce as possible.

Bringing up the Babies

An owl lays an egg every two or three days until the **clutch** is complete. This means that the eggs will hatch at the same intervals. There may be two weeks or more between the time that the first and last eggs hatch, so the

A great horned owl guards its chicks. When they are larger, the chicks will be left alone, so both parents can go hunting.

oldest chick is much bigger than the youngest.

When owl chicks hatch, their eyes and ears are closed. They have only a thin coat of down and they cannot keep warm on their own. The female owl continues to keep them warm until they have grown a thicker coat of down. Then she can leave the nest and help the male to bring food.

With a rapidly growing family, both parents have to work hard to catch enough prey to satisfy the chicks' hunger. While they are very young, the female tears up prey and gives the chicks strips of meat to swallow, but they soon grow big enough to swallow mice and other animals whole.

Young owls leave the nest when they are about a month old. They take a week to learn to fly well and then start to hunt for themselves, but they still need to be fed by their parents. Young tawny owls spend about three months hunting in their parents' territory. Once they can fend for themselves, young owls have to find their own territories because there will not be enough food if they remain with their parents.

These young burrowing owls are nearly ready to fly. They have come out of the burrow to exercise their wings and explore their surroundings.

The Survival of Owls

The number of owls that can live in one place is controlled by the amount of prey animals living there. If prey is scarce, the owls will have smaller families. A shortage of food means that they will lay fewer eggs and some of their chicks may not survive.

Because the eggs in an owl's nest hatch at different times, some chicks are larger than others. The older and stronger chicks are fed first. When the parent owl arrives with food, they push the younger chicks out of the way. The young ones are fed only when the older chicks are full. If there is a shortage of food, only the older chicks get enough, and the younger ones eventually die of starvation.

So, when prey is scarce, the owls produce one or two healthy chicks instead of several half-starved ones. A healthy chick has a better chance of surviving when it leaves the nest and has to learn to look after itself. Half-starved chicks have no chance of surviving.

If there is a shortage of food, the older and stronger of these barn owl chicks will survive, but the smaller ones will not be fed and may starve to death.

Many young owls die during their first winter, but those that do survive will nest in the following spring and will probably live for several years. Eagle owls have lived for over 50 years

A young great-horned owl spreads its wings to scare off an enemy.

in captivity, but wild owls rarely live for more than 10 years.

5
Owls and People

Owls fly near the ground when they are hunting. When they fly across a road they are often killed by vehicles.

Owls in Danger

Some species of owls are becoming rare. People sometimes kill owls because they think that the owls hunt pheasants and other **gamebirds**. Sometimes owls are even shot for fun.

Killing owls is a serious problem but there is a greater danger. Changes in the landscape have destroyed the owls' nesting places and their hunting grounds. When this happens owls may disappear completely. If a wood is cut down and turned into fields for growing crops, or if it is cleared for houses and roads, there will be no trees for the owls to nest in. The animals they eat will also disappear. Unless the owls can find somewhere else to live, they will die.

Another serious problem is poisoning with **pesticides**. These are chemicals that are sprayed onto fields and forests to kill insect pests. The insects are poisoned when they eat plants that have been treated with the pesticides. The insects are then eaten by birds or mammals. Finally owls eat the birds and mammals, or the insects, and are also poisoned. The birds and mammals pick up the poison from the many insects they eat, and the owls pick up poison from them. So the poisons are concentrated at each stage and the owls receive enough poison to kill them.

Even birdwatchers can harm owls accidentally. Owls are very shy when they start to lay their eggs, and they may abandon the nest if disturbed by people who come too close.

Farmers spray fields of wheat with pesticide to kill harmful insects. The shoots are eaten by voles, which are then hunted by owls. The owls therefore receive a large dose of pesticide, which is often enough to kill them.

The Future of Owls

The slaughter of owls has been prevented in many countries by passing laws to protect these birds. It is more difficult to save owls from the destruction of the countryside, but many people are trying to help by providing nesting places and preserving the owls' hunting grounds.

When old trees are cut down, owls lose their nesting places and they have to try to find somewhere else to live.

Foresters cut down old, rotten trees because they encourage insect pests. These are the trees that owls like for their nests. In Sweden and Finland, nestboxes have been put up in woods to replace the lost natural nesting places. As a result, the number of Ural owls has increased. The Dutch have persuaded barn owls to nest in boxes placed in the roofs of farm buildings.

Modern farms often consist of huge fields of crops and there are fewer patches of rough grass where mice and voles live. **Conservationists** in Britain are persuading landowners to leave strips of uncultivated ground around their fields and along the banks of rivers. This will provide enough hunting ground for barn owls.

A number of owl species have taken to living in towns and villages in different parts of the world. Tawny owls, Ural owls, hawk owls, scops owls and screech owls have become

Tawny owls often live in towns and villages and hunt in gardens.

town dwellers where there are parks and large gardens. Little owls and barn owls sometimes join the other urban owls in new suburbs, where there are plenty of open spaces and old trees for them to use.

6
Learning More about Owls

Patience, care and good luck are needed to study owls.

Looking for Owls

Most owls are active at night when people are indoors, so they are not as easy to watch as other birds. You may see owls lit up by car headlights as they perch on posts by the roadside.

The easiest owls to spot are those that come out in the early evening. Little owls perch on branches, fence posts and telegraph poles. Barn owls and short-eared owls fly over grassy meadows. A winter afternoon is a good time to see them.

The mainly brown plumage makes an owl very difficult to see when it is roosting, but its position is given away when small birds gather around and scold it with harsh cries. This form of bird behavior is called mobbing, and it shows all the birds in the neighborhood where a **predator** is hiding.

After an owl has had a meal, it

brings up the indigestible bones, fur and feathers as a pellet. Searching for pellets around the bases of large trees or in old buildings is a good way of finding owl roosts and nests. The pellets contain evidence of what the owls have been eating.

If you want to find out, soak the pellets in a jar of water for several hours, shaking it occasionally. Skim off the fur and feathers that float to the top. Repeat this several times and pour the remains into a dish. The bones and pieces of insect shells can be carefully lifted out with tweezers.

This pellet came from an owl that had eaten a rodent. You can see one of its jaw bones.

The saw-whet owl gets its name from its call, which sounds like someone sharpening, or whetting, a saw.

Listening for Owls

Although owls are not easy to see, they can be heard over long distances. They are noisiest in the spring. By quietly following their calls, it may be possible to get near enough to see them. It is even possible to get owls to come near by imitating their calls. The owl thinks there is a rival in its territory and investigates. However, it is unwise to alarm the owl if it is close to you.

The calls of owls are often called "hoots." This is a good description of the "whoo-oo" of a tawny owl or the slow "boo-boo-boo" of a short-eared owl, but other owls produce a variety of sounds. Barn owls have a long scream and the little owl calls "kew-kew."

These calls are the owls' "songs." Like the musical songs of other birds, they are used to show that the owl has

a territory and is looking for a mate. Sometimes the female answers and the pair sing in a duet.

Owls also call for other reasons. "Kewick" calls keep male and female tawny owls in touch with each other.

You may hear the barn owls loud, scary shrieks when you are out in the country.

A sneezing call tells adult tawny owls the position of their chicks after they have left the nest.

Glossary

Birds of prey Birds that have curved beaks and talons for catching prey. They include owls, eagles, hawks and falcons.

Clutch A set of eggs laid in a nest.

Conservationists People who work to protect (or conserve) animals and the places they live in.

Gamebird A bird that is shot for sport. Pheasants, partridges and grouse are gamebirds.

Incubated Kept warm by the parent bird in the nest.

Migrate Travel between winter and summer homes.

Nocturnal Coming out at night, and resting during the day.

Ornithologists People who study birds.

Pesticides Poisons used for killing insects and other animals that harm crops.

Plumage A bird's coat of feathers.

Predator An animal that preys on other animals.

Pupil The round "window" that lets light into the eye.

Retina A light-sensitive layer at the back of the eyball.

Rodents Small mammals such as rats, mice, voles, lemmings and squirrels.

Species A particular kind of animal or plant. The tawny owl, barn owl and snowy owl are different species of owls.

Talons The sharp claws of a bird of prey.

Territory An area that an animal defends against other animals

Finding Out More

If you would like to find out more about owls, you might read the following books:

Birds of Prey by Kate Petty. Gloucester, 1987

Birds by Carolyn Boulton. Franklin Watts, 1984

Discovering Birds of Prey by Mike Thomas and Eric Soothill. Bookwright, 1986

Eagles, Hawks, and Other Birds of Prey by Linda DeWitt. Franklin Watts, 1989

Hunting and Stalking by Malcolm Penny. Bookwright, 1988

The Life Cycle of an Owl by Jill Bailey. Bookwright, 1990

The Owl in the Tree by Jennifer Coldrey. Stevens, Inc., 1987

Picture Acknowledgments

All photographs from Oxford Scientific Films by the following photographers: M. Austerman (Animals Animals) 24; L.M. Crowhurst 10; E.R. Degging (Animals Animals) 34; John Gerlach (Animals Animals) 33; Mark Hamblin 19, 43; Steffen Hauser 12; Terry Heathcote 38; Michael Leach 11, 21, 22, 36, 39, 41; Leonard Lee Rue III (Animals Animals) *frontispiece*; Ted Levin (Animals Animals) 14, 31; Joe McDonald (Animals Animals) 40, 42; N.J. Millington/Richard Kolar (Animals Animals) 23; Muzz Murray 9, 16; Stan Osolinski 8, 29; Charles Palek (Animals Animals) 26, 32, 35; D.J. Saunders *cover*; Alastair Shay 20; David Thompson 13, 18; Barrie E. Watts 27; Graham J. Wren 30. The illustrations are by Wendy Meadway.

Index

The numbers in **bold** refer to the pictures.